Animal Diaries
Life Cycles

A Kangaroo's Life

by
Ellen Lawrence

Consultants:

Suzy Gazlay, MA
Recipient, Presidential Award for Excellence in Science Teaching

Stella Reid
Wildhaven Wildlife Shelter, St Andrews, Victoria, Australia

Kimberly Brenneman, PhD
National Institute for Early Education Research, Rutgers University, New Brunswick, New Jersey

BEARPORT
PUBLISHING

New York, New York

Credits

Cover, © Frans Lanting/FLPA; cover L, © Superstock; I, © Superstock; 2, © Smileus/Shutterstock; 4T, © Ivanna Matson/Superstock; 4B, © Cosmographics; 5, © Jurgen & Christine Sohns/FLPA; 6, © C. Huetter/Alamy; 7, © Mitsuaki Iwago/FLPA; 8, © A.N.T. Photo Library/NHPA; 9, © Steve Downer/Ardea; II, © Mitsuaki Iwago/FLPA; I2, © Mitsuaki Iwago/FLPA; I3, © Belinda Images/Superstock; I4, © Tier und Naturfotografie/Superstock; I5, © Tier und Naturfotografie/Superstock; I6, © Owen Newman/Naturepl; I7, © Elizabeth C. Doerner/Shutterstock; I8T, © Mitsuaki Iwago/FLPA; I9, © Jurgen & Christine Sohns/FLPA; 20, © Mitsuaki Iwago/FLPA; 2I, © Gerard Lacz/FLPA; 22, © Eric Isselée/Shutterstock; 23TL, © Smileus/Shutterstock; 23TR, © C. Huetter/Alamy; 23 BL, © Tier und Naturfotografie/Superstock; 23BC, © Lisa Maree Williams/Getty Images; 23BR, © Gerard Lacz/FLPA; 24, © Eric Isselée.

Publisher: Kenn Goin
Senior Editor: Lisa Wiseman
Creative Director: Spencer Brinker
Design: Alix Wood
Editor: Mark J. Sachner
Photo Researcher: Ruby Tuesday Books Ltd

Library of Congress Cataloging-in-Publication Data

Lawrence, Ellen, I967–
  A kangaroo's life / By Ellen Lawrence.
    p. cm. — (Animal diaries: Life cycles)
  Includes bibliographical references and index.
  ISBN 978-I-6I772-4I5-2 (library binding)—ISBN I-6I772-4I5-7 (library binding)
  I. Kangaroos—Life cycles—Juvenile literature. I. Title.
  QL737.M35L39 20I2
  599.2'22—dc23

                                   20II044727

For more information, write to Bearport Publishing Company, Inc., 45 West 2Ist Street, Suite 3B, New York, New York I00I0. Printed in the United States of America in North Mankato, Minnesota.

I0 9 8 7 6 5 4 3 2 I

Contents

Name: **David**   Date: **September 1**

Fighting Kangaroos!

Today, I saw two red kangaroos having a fight!

I live in Australia, and lots of kangaroos live near my family's farm.

My Aunt Annie knows a lot about kangaroos because she's a **veterinarian**.

Aunt Annie said the kangaroos were males.

They were fighting over who would get to **mate** with the females.

David

Where red kangaroos live in the wild

4

Red kangaroos live in the **wild** in Australia. They live in dry, open places where there are bushes, grass, and only a few trees.

red kangaroos fighting

Imagine one of your friends has never seen a kangaroo. Describe what a kangaroo looks like to your friend.

5

Date: **October 13**

A Lucky Baby

Yesterday, on the road near our farm, a car hit a female kangaroo.

She was taken to the animal rescue center where Aunt Annie works.

Aunt Annie looked her over and said that the animal was not hurt badly.

She also said that the kangaroo was carrying a baby just a few days old.

The tiny creature was safe and cozy inside his mother's furry **pouch**.

male kangaroo

pouch

female kangaroo

A baby kangaroo is called a **joey**. A newborn joey is the size of a jellybean!

a newborn joey inside its mother's pouch

Pick up a dime and feel how much it weighs. A newborn joey weighs less than a dime!

Date: **October 20**

A Tiny Joey

Today, I visited the mother kangaroo at the rescue center.

Aunt Annie showed me the tiny joey inside his mother's pouch.

He is now about ten days old.

The joey's eyes are closed, and he cannot see.

The little baby has lots of growing to do before he can leave the pouch.

a joey inside its mother's pouch

A female kangaroo gives birth to her first joey when she is about three years old.

one-week-old joey

How does a joey look different from an adult kangaroo?

Date: **November 7**

Growing Bigger

The joey is now about four weeks old.

He is nearly four inches (10 cm) long.

Safe inside the pouch, the joey drinks milk from his mother.

Today, I saw the mother kangaroo licking inside her pouch.

Aunt Annie says that kangaroo moms clean their joeys up to seven times a day.

When a joey goes to the bathroom, the mother licks up its waste to keep the joey and the pouch clean.

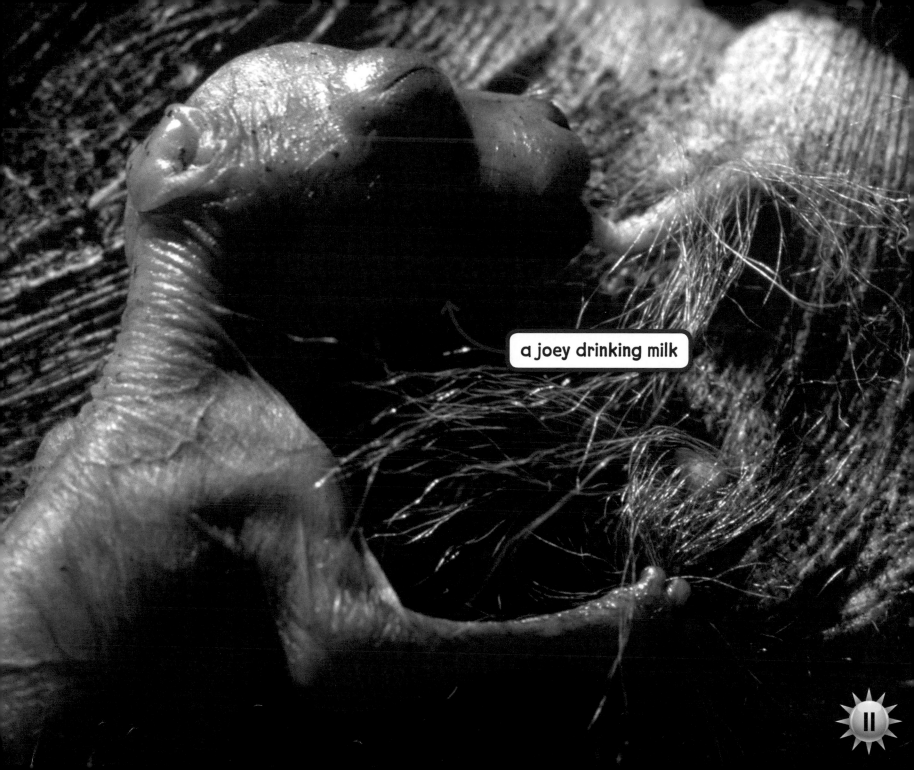

a joey drinking milk

Date: **February 27**

Hello, Joey!

As the joey grew bigger, I could see him wriggling around in the pouch!

Aunt Annie told me that joeys open their eyes when they are about 16 weeks old.

Then their fur starts to grow.

Today, after 20 weeks, the moment I've been waiting for arrived.

The joey popped his head out of his mom's pouch for the first time!

15-week-old joey inside its mother's pouch

When a joey first begins to pop its head out of its mother's pouch, it will sometimes try to take a nibble of grass while its mother is bending over to feed.

a joey looking out of its mother's pouch

Date: **March 2**

Time to Leave Home!

This morning the mother kangaroo was eating grass.

The little joey wanted to eat some, too.

He reached his head farther and farther out of the pouch.

Then—plop! The joey tumbled onto the ground.

It was the joey's first time outside!

He hopped around for a minute, then climbed back into the safety of his mother's pouch.

joey

pouch

Date: **June 8**

A Big Joey

The joey is now eight months old.

He doesn't live in his mother's pouch anymore.

He is too big.

He still drinks milk from his mother, however.

When he wants a drink, he sticks his head inside the pouch!

a mother kangaroo and her joey cuddling

After a joey leaves the pouch, it still drinks milk from its mother for about four months.

a joey drinking milk

Date: **October 16**

Back to the Wild

The joey and his mother lived at the rescue center for a while longer.

After a year, the mother kangaroo was feeling healthy and strong again.

Aunt Annie helped return the mother and her joey to the wild.

There, they live with other kangaroos near our farm.

The joey is now a year old, and he eats grass and small plants, just like his mother.

Kangaroos live in small groups called mobs. There are usually about 6 to 30 kangaroos in a mob.

a mob of kangaroos drinking

mother kangaroo

joey

Date: **October 20**

Growing Up

Today, I saw the joey hopping along with his mother and some other kangaroos.

He is growing bigger and stronger, but it will be another year before he is an adult.

Then he will weigh nearly 200 pounds (91 kg), and he will be 6 feet (1.83 m) tall!

Maybe one day I'll see him fighting with another male over who will get to mate with the females.

adult male kangaroo

Kangaroos move by hopping from place to place. An adult kangaroo can cover up to 26 feet (8 m) in a single hop.

a mob of
kangaroos hopping

Choose a starting point. Then measure 26 feet (8 m) and put down a marker. Make the longest jumps that you can. How many jumps does it take you to jump the same distance as one kangaroo hop?

21

Science Lab

Make a chart like the one below. In it, list the things that are the same and different about a kangaroo joey and your favorite baby animal.

A Baby Chimpanzee and a Joey

Things that are the same:	Things that are different:
They are both mammals.	A chimpanzee is not a marsupial.
They both have fur.	A baby chimp doesn't grow in a pouch.
Their moms carry them around.	A chimp doesn't have a tail.

Find information about your favorite animal using books or the Internet. Include the information on your chart.

———— Fact File ————

Marsupials

Kangaroos belong to a group of animals called marsupials.

Kangaroos, wallabies, koalas, and opossums are all marsupials.

Marsupials are mammals, which means they are warm-blooded, have a backbone, and have hair or fur.

Mammals give birth to live babies and feed their babies milk from their bodies.

Marsupials are different from other mammals because they give birth to very tiny babies that are not fully formed.

A marsupial baby finishes growing inside its mother's pouch, instead of inside her body.

koala

Science Words

joey (JOH-ee) the name for a baby animal that is carried in a pouch by its mother; baby kangaroos, wallabies, and koalas are all called joeys

mate (MAYT) to come together in order to have young

pouch (POUCH) part of a mother kangaroo's belly used for carrying her young

veterinarian (*vet*-ur-uh-NER-ee-uhn) a doctor who cares for animals

wild (WILDE) large outdoor areas in nature where animals can live and travel freely

Index

Read More

Bredeson, Carmen. *Kangaroos Up Close (Zoom in on Animals!).* Berkeley Heights, NJ: Enslow Publishers, Inc. (2012).

Lunis, Natalie. *Red Kangaroo: The World's Largest Marsupial. (More Supersized).* New York: Bearport (2010).

Swanson, Diane. *Kangaroos (Welcome to the World).* Vancouver: Whitecap Books (2010).

Learn More Online

To learn more about kangaroos, visit **www.bearportpublishing.com/AnimalDiaries**

About the Author

Ellen Lawrence lives in the United Kingdom. Her favorite books to write are those about animals. In fact, the first book Ellen bought for herself, when she was six years old, was the story of a gorilla named Patty Cake that was born in New York's Central Park Zoo.